TYF*planner*™

Published by Tinu Publishing, LLC

2022 USA

TYF*Planner*™
Contents

Introduction

Did you know? Studies have shown that taking small actions daily lead to significant overall results. The TYF*planner*™ is designed to **TRANSFORM YOUR FINANCES IN 28 DAYS** by completing daily "small actions." Each action comes with tips to help you complete the action.

HOW TO BEST USE THIS PLANNER

- Complete the small action for each day.
- Write any learnings, follow ups, or questions you have in the space provided.
- Join the conversation and become part of a community of people also transforming their finances. www.dailymoneyactions.com

01

PHASE

Build a Foundation

Weeks 1 through 4 are dedicated to building a solid financial foundation. Topics covered:

- Cash Flow
- Reducing Expenses
- Emergency Fund
- Eliminating Debt

Cash Flow

Your cash flow is money flowing in (income) minus money flowing out (Expenses). Your financial foundation begins with knowing and monitoring your Cash Flow.

Sunday

Sunday is a good day to be intentional for the upcoming week. As this week begins, be intentional about making the time to complete each small action and to learn, share and engage with others. Money conversations helps us learn new things.

This week's focus is Cash Flow.

> Think of all the ways money flow in and out for you. Do you have a good way to monitor, track and react? List the instances where you do not or are unable to monitor, track, react.

TIP: Don't forget cash transactions!

Monday

> Review how much money you spent the previous month.

Were there any surprises? Is it hard to know exactly how much you spent? Why?

TIP: Take a look at credit card and bank statements.

Tuesday

> Select or explore a spending tracker that meets your needs.

Already use one: Is it meeting your needs? Is there a better app/system for you?

TIP: A spreadsheet might also do the trick!

Wednesday

> Review all money coming in (income) from the previous month.

Are you able to track it all? Any surprises?

TIP: Use bank statements and pay stubs for accuracy

Thursday

> Set a reminder to review your cash flow (money in, money out) at a frequency of your choosing.

Will you review daily, weekly or monthly?

TIP: Do what works for you and commit to it!

Friday

> What was the biggest challenge you faced? What actions do you still need to complete?

TIP: Reflect on the small actions for the week

Saturday

> Celebrate 🥂 Share your success stories, eye openers and confirmations from this week with your cheerleaders!

TIP: Small wins are worth celebrating!

Week - 01

Summary

Awesome outcomes you achieved in week 1

02 WEEK

Reduce Expenses

When thinking of expenses, think of all the times money leaves your pocket, wallet, or account. Some expenses are fixed, while others might be variable or periodic.

Sunday

Sunday is a good day to be intentional for the upcoming week. As this week begins, be intentional about making the time to complete each small action and to learn, share and engage with others. Money conversations helps us learn new things.

This week's focus is Reduce Expenses.

> Think of all the ways money flows in and out for you. Do you have a good way to monitor, track and react? List the instances where you do not or are unable to monitor, track, react.

TIP: Don't forget cash transactions!

Monday

Categorize your expenses into these 5 buckets.

- Taxes & Deductions
- Fixed Expenses
- Variable Expenses
- Periodic Expenses
- Discretionary Expenses

Tip: Fixed expenses don't change from month to month while variable expenses do. Periodic expenses may occur annually or quarterly.

Join the conversation: www.dailymoneyactions.com

Tuesday

Groceries aka the Budget buster!

Review your grocery spending for last month. What can you change?

TIP: Make your spending more visible by dedicating an account to grocery/household spending only.

Wednesday

> Set a budget for each expense category.

TIP: An average of the past 3 months for each category is a good place to start. Refine as needed.

Thursday

> Automate expenses. Start with fixed expenses.

TIP: Because fixed expenses don't change, they are the best category for automation.

Friday

> What was the biggest challenge you faced? What actions do you still need to complete?

TIP: Reflect on the small actions for the week

Saturday

> Celebrate 🥂 Share your success stories, eye openers and confirmations from this week with your cheerleaders!

TIP: Small wins are worth celebrating!

Week - 02

Summary

Awesome outcomes you achieved in week 2

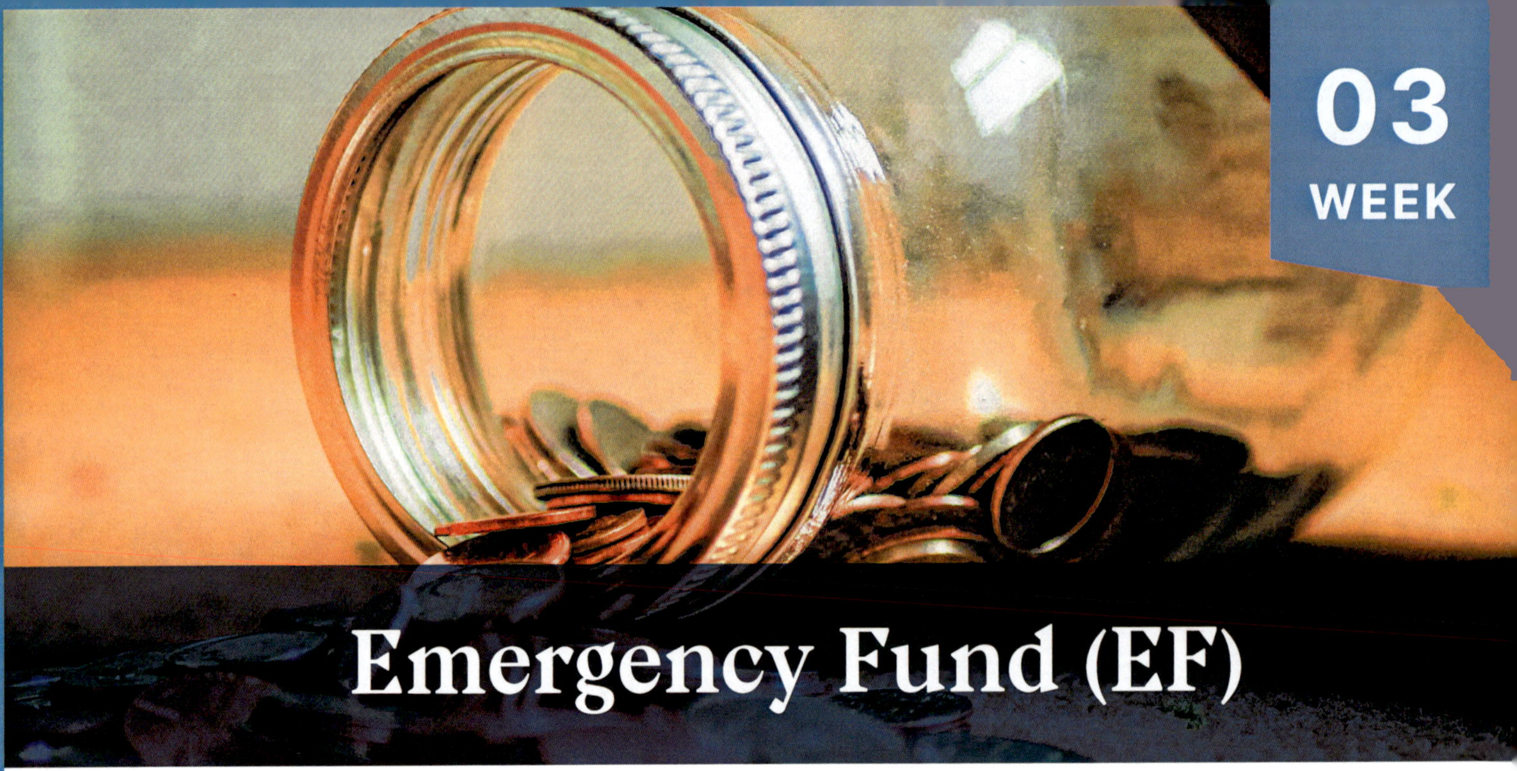

03
WEEK

Emergency Fund (EF)

Being intentional goes a long way in taking action and accomplishing goals.

As this week kicks off, be intentional about making the time to complete each small action, to learn, share and engage with others.

By the end of this week you will:

- Understand your emergency fund needs.
- Make a plan to adequately fund your emergency fund.
- Know where to stash your emergency fund and how to replenish it.

Sunday

It's going to be a great week! Set your intention now to make it a reality.

HINT: Sundays are also great for reviewing the previous week and completing unfinished actions.

Monday

Calculate your EF numbers.

Know your 3 EF numbers.

1. Expenses you need to cover
2. Number of months EF will cover
3. Total EF $ (#1 multiplied by #2)

TIP: Use what you learned about your expenses from last week. Target a minimum of 3 months.

Tuesday

Make a plan to fund your EF with the amount you need.

TIP: Keep your EF in a separate account. An online bank with high yields is ideal.

Wednesday

> Decide where you will stash your Emergency Fund.

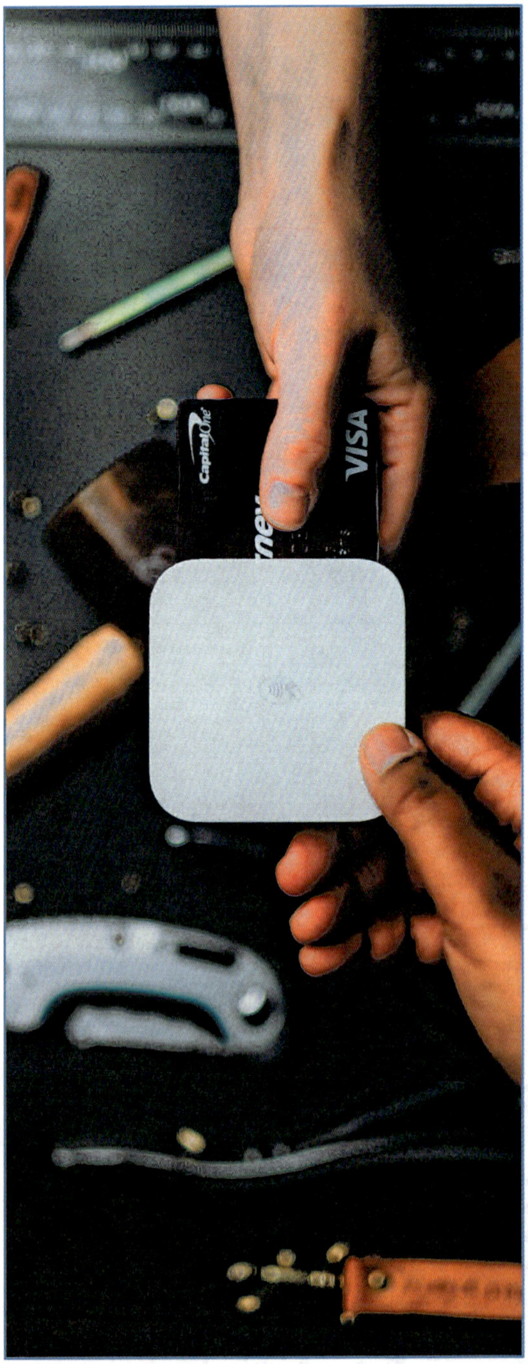

TIP: Choose the account that best works for you

1. **High-Yield Savings Account**
   A high-yield savings account is reasonably accessible and allows you to receive a higher interest rate than a traditional savings account.

2. **Money Market Account**
   Money market accounts sometimes come with a debit card and check-writing capabilities, making them more convenient, especially in a pinch. Money market accounts generally require a larger minimum deposit to open an account. You can open a money market account at most local banks, as well as online banks.

3. **Certificate of Deposit**
   Certificates of Deposit (CDs) are another possibility for your emergency fund. They are different from other options on this list because they require you to keep your money in the account for a specific period of time in exchange for receiving a guaranteed rate of return.

4. **Traditional Bank Account**
   You can always keep your emergency fund in a traditional checking or savings account with a brick-and-mortar bank. You won't earn as much interest, but you have the peace of mind that comes from knowing you can access your funds at any time.

Thursday

> Define the emergencies you expect your EF to address.

Here are some of the top emergencies people face:

- Job loss.
- Medical or dental emergency.
- Unexpected home repairs.
- Car troubles.
- Unplanned travel expenses.

TIP: Focus on the emergencies that are most likely for your situation.

Friday

> What was the biggest challenge you faced? What actions do you still need to complete?

TIP: Reflect on the small actions for the week

Saturday

> Celebrate 🥂 Share your success stories, eye openers and confirmations from this week with your cheerleaders!

TIP: Small wins are worth celebrating!

Week - 03

Summary

Awesome outcomes you achieved in week 3

04
WEEK

Eliminate Debt

Eliminating or reducing your debt frees up cash that you can use towards your financial goals.

Sunday

Being intentional goes a long way in accomplishing goals.

> As this week kicks off, be intentional about making the time to complete each small action and engage with others.

By the end of this week you will:

- Understand and categorize your current debt
- Make a plan to eliminate one or more categories of debt
- Identify strategies and a plan to avoid new debt

It's going to be a great week! Set your intention now to make it a reality.

HINT: Sundays are also great for reviewing the previous week

Monday

> Review your current debt and categorize them into the 4 main debt categories.

The 4 main categories of debt are:

1. Secured debt
2. Unsecured debt
3. Revolving debt
4. Mortgages

TIP: Join the conversation to learn more about debt categories www.dailymoneyactions.com

Tuesday

> Focus on your revolving debt. What steps can you take to completely eliminate it?

TIP: Revolving debt tend to have the highest interest rate

Wednesday

Go SHOPPING!

When last did you review the rates on your other 3 categories of debt (unsecured, secured and mortgage)? Do you have the best rate? Can you get a lower rate?

Lower rate = lower total interest paid and lower monthly payment.

This can mean paying down the debt faster with extra payments.

TIP: Use online rate comparison sites like Bankrate

Thursday

Write down 5 ways you will avoid new debt AND share it with someone.

TIP: An accountability partner can help ensure you stay on track.

Friday

“ What was the biggest challenge you faced? What actions do you still need to complete?

TIP: Reflect on the small actions for the week

Saturday

“ Celebrate 🥂 Share your success stories, eye openers and confirmations from this week with your cheerleaders!

TIP: Small wins are worth celebrating!

Week - 04

Summary

Awesome outcomes you achieved in week 4

02

PHASE

Advanced Builder

Phase 2 focuses on topics that build on the foundation established in Phase 1, and consists of weeks 5 through 7.

At the end of Phase 2 you will establish:

- A plan for increasing your income
- Specific retirement strategies to maximize contributions and the types of accounts that meet your needs
- A comprehensive financial plan that identifies short, medium and long term actions that will ensure you meet your financial goals.

05
WEEK

Retirement Planning

Whether you dream of early retirement or plan to go the more traditional route, you need a plan to ensure an enjoyable retirement!

At the end of this week you will:

- Identify the different retirement plans available to you
- Learn tips for selecting the appropriate investments
- Determine your retirement number and goals

Sunday

Sunday is a good day to be intentional for the upcoming week. As this week kicks off, be intentional about making the time to complete each small action and to learn, share and engage with others.

HINT: Sundays are also great for reviewing the previous week

Monday

Determine your retirement numbers!

Determine these 2 numbers:

1. Number of years before desired retirement
2. Desired monthly income in retirement

TIP: take the time to envision your ideal retirement.

Tuesday

Know the type of retirement plan(s) you have.

The most common retirement plans are:

1. 401(k)
2. 403(b)
3. 457
4. IRA

TIP: Join the conversation to learn more about different retirement plans www.dailymoneyactions.com

Wednesday

> Understand your retirement plan and get the most out of it

TIP: 7 tips to help with today's small action:

1. Select the right contribution rate, don't just go with the default (typically 3%!)
2. Ensure you are getting ALL the employer match. It isn't free money it is part of your compensation!Read your plan documents, there may be other ways to get additional match contributions from your employer e.g. if your employer matches annual bonus contributions.
3. Understand the vesting schedule for your plan. It can weigh in on some decisions e.g. the decision to leave.
4. See what types of accounts your company has made available to you. For example, do they allow after-tax contributions? This can really help you super size your retirement planning.
5. Does your company have a pension or other non elective contribution that is made on your behalf? If you don't know the answer, ask HR!
6. What free financial services come with your plan? Take advantage of them! Call to discuss investment allocation or a portfolio review.
7. Prioritize paying off any retirement plan loans and be careful about taking future loans from your plan.

Thursday

Optimize your retirement investments.

Review the investments in your retirement accounts (include taxable accounts if they are part of your retirement planning).

Low cost index funds or ETFs remain the best investing strategy for most people.

TIP: Compare similar funds by their Expense Ratio. Expense Ratio is the cost of a fund expressed as a %.

Friday

What was the biggest challenge you faced? What actions do you still need to complete?

TIP: Reflect on the small actions for the week

Saturday

Celebrate 🥂 Share your success stories, eye openers and confirmations from this week with your cheerleaders!

TIP: Small wins are worth celebrating!

Week - 05

Summary

Awesome outcomes you achieved in week 5

06 WEEK

Increase Income

Sunday

Sunday is a great day to be intentional about setting goals for the upcoming week.
As this week kicks off, be intentional about making the time to complete each small action and to learn, share and engage with others.

By the end of this week you will understand:

- Your current sources of income and which ones you can increase
- Opportunities and strategies you can adopt to increase your current income
- Opportunities you can explore to increase your number of income sources

> Set your intention now to get in the right mindset for the week.

Hint: Sundays are also great for reviewing the previous week and unfinished actions

Monday

> Review your income and categorize into the 7 income sources.

The 7 Categories of income are:

1. Earned income
2. Business income
3. Interest income
4. Dividend income
5. Rental income
6. Capital gains
7. Royalties/licensing

TIP: Join the conversation to learn more about the 7 income sources www.dailymoneyactions.com

Tuesday

> Visualize your worth.
> Create a vision board.

A vision board is a powerful tool for visualizing and accomplishing goals. How do you want to increase your income? Visualize it using pictures that represent your goal.

TIP: Keep your vision board in a very visible area

Wednesday

> Make a plan to transform your vision board from vision to reality.

TIP: For each item on your vision board write at least one goal and an accompanying action

Thursday

> Identify 3 things you can do to improve your health.

A study: Poor health contributes to reduced income, referred to as the health-poverty trap.

TIP: Health really is wealth!

Friday

“ What was the biggest challenge you faced? What actions do you still need to complete?

TIP: Reflect on the small actions for the week

Saturday

“ Celebrate 🥂 Share your success stories, eye openers and confirmations from this week with your cheerleaders!

TIP: Small wins are worth celebrating!

Week - 06

Summary

Awesome outcomes you achieved in week 6

07
WEEK

Financial Plan

Formalize all the work from the previous weeks by creating a written financial plan.

Being intentional goes a long way in taking action and accomplishing goals.
As this week kicks off, be intentional about making the time to complete each small action and to learn, share and engage with others.

By the end of this week you will:

- Understand how to create a financial plan
- Define the elements of your financial plan
- Create your initial financial plan
- Review and update your financial plan to keep it relevant and up to date

Sunday

It's going to be a great week! Set your intention now to make it a reality.

HINT: Sundays are also great for reviewing the previous week and completing unfinished actions

Monday

Identify 3-5 financial goals.

Don't hold back. Think of your WIGs (Wildly Important Goals) and BHAGs (Big Hairy Audacious Goals)

TIP: Write them down!

Tuesday

Refine your 3-5 financial goals by making them S.M.A.R.T

- **Specific**
- **Measurable**
- **Attainable**
- **Relevant**
- **Time-bound**

TIP: Join the conversation about creating SMART goals www.dailymoneyactions.com

Wednesday

> Define the "how" for each financial goal you identified.

Now that you've identified (and written) your financial goals, it's time to determine what actions will help you accomplish them.

It's ok to not have all the answers yet but it's important to continue to think of (and refine) the actions that will support your goals.

TIP: Revisit and refine your goals as often as you need.

Thursday

> Identify the potential risks to your "how" for each financial goal.

This is the final step in creating your Financial Plan.

After identifying how you plan to accomplish your goals, it is important to also think of situations that will prevent you from completing the actions as planned.

TIP: For each risk identify a way to mitigate risks

Friday

> What was the biggest challenge you faced?
> What actions do you still need to complete?

TIP: Reflect on the small actions for the week

Saturday

> Celebrate 🥂 Share your success stories, eye openers and confirmations from this week with your cheerleaders!

TIP: Small wins are worth celebrating!

Week - 07

Summary

Awesome outcomes you achieved in week 7

CONGRATS!

Continue the conversation

www.dailymoneyactions.com

Additional resources:

www.fiwoman.com

Made in United States
North Haven, CT
05 November 2026

21763976R00027